THE RUSSIAN IDEA

The Russian Idea

Vladimir Solovyov
Владимир Сергеевич Соловьёв

Translated by Fr. John P. Rickert, FSSP

ISBN: 1508510075
ISBN 13: 9781508510079
Library of Congress Control Number: 2015902567
CreateSpace Independent Publishing Platform
North Charleston, South Carolina

Reginae Matrique Carissimae
– The Translator

INTRODUCTION

THE PRESENT ESSAY of Solovyov represents a kind of writing not common these days, intermingling theology, the theological meaning of history, and the theological sense of the identity and providential destiny of a nation or people. St. Augustine attempted this in his *City of God* and Padre Antônio Vieira, S.J., in his *Clavis Prophetarum*. In a similar vein, Juan Donoso Cortés considered the political order from a theological standpoint in his *Essay on Catholicism, Liberalism, and Socialism*. Such an endeavor now may seem impossible, or at least worthy of derision, to the current-day mind, which sees countries and peoples as merely arbitrary, and therefore arbitrarily mutable, *congeries* having no true substantial identity, and the human and social order as worlds sufficient unto themselves not bound by any higher law or divine Providence.

Yet, it is better for me not say much, to let the reader discern for himself, and to focus here instead on certain salient points regarding the translation. For some studies of Solovyov and his thought, please the section entitled **Further Reading.**

<hr>

The French text used is that found on the website "Bibliothèque russe et slave" (http://bibliotheque-russe-et-slave.com/index1.html), which incorporates into the body of the text the corrigenda found on p. 47 of the 1888 Perrin edition of this essay. The Perrin edition itself is directly available on books.google.com. When Solovyov quotes another work, e.g., the Bible, I have simply translated his French text as it stands, without comparing it to its original. While I have tried to avoid adding text, most of the times where I have done so, or where I quote the original, I use [square brackets]. For footnotes, those with numbers in parentheses, e.g., "(1)" indicate a footnote and its numbering in the edition of the essay on the Bibliothèque russe et slave. Footnotes without parenthetical numbering have been added by the translator.

<hr>

Solovyov uses the word *organique* at a number of key points. In contrast to current usage, in which "organic" has come to be synonymous with "natural, not artificial," Solovyov's use of the word is true to its origins: an organ is a vital, functioning, integrated part of a larger whole that serves a specific function, as, for example, eyes are the organ of sight – such is their purpose, and no other part of the body has this purpose – and the ears are organs of hearing – such is their purpose, and no other part of the body has this purpose. What organ, then, in this sense, is Russia, not for the secular and passing world, but for the incarnate body of Christ on Earth, as envisioned by the supernatural order of divine Providence? This is the question which Solovyov attempts to answer.

Perhaps the most difficult question of translation regards the title itself. It is well known that Russian often converts into adjectives what we in English often express by nouns or noun phrases. Is the best translation of the title of this work "The Russian Idea," or "The Idea of Russia" or "Russia's Idea," or something else? It is clear that Solovyov is not simply enucleating and elucidating what is simply a tacitly held idea by the mass of his countrymen, which argues against the first and third of the three proposals. Yet there remains the sense that this essay is put forward as a uniquely and distinctively Russian idea, divinely commissioned, to the world. As for the second proposal, Solovyov's aspiration reaches beyond any boundaries that the nation of Russia may have. Hence, it is not accurate to entitle this work as "The Idea of Russia," either, as if the present essay were a prescription specially designated for his own country, or a call to live up to a certain identity that others are not called to share in. Solovyov envisions that a nation finds it true identity precisely in fulfilling its divinely given mission and function; for which reason the title of this essay could have been, it seems to me, "The Divino-Russian Idea."

I am very grateful for all the help and encouragement I have received, especially for the dogged persistence of John Watkins. Great thanks to my Superior General, Fr. John Berg, FSSP, for his permission to proceed with this project. Very great thanks to my parents. And above all thanks to God for His Providence and blessings.

Solovyov's Preface

THE PURPOSE OF these pages is not to give details over the current state of Russia, as if it were a country unknown or badly known in the West.

Without speaking of the numerous translations which have familiarized Europe with the masterpieces of our literature, one sees now, especially in France, some eminent writers who are informing the European public about Russia; very much better, perhaps, than a Russian himself would know how. To name but two Frenchmen, Anatole Leroy-Beaulieu has given, in his excellent work, *The Empire of the Tsars*, an exposition that is quite true to the facts, quite complete, and quite well done, of the state of our politics, society, and religion; and the viscount de Vogüe, in a series of brilliant writings on Russian literature, has treated his subject not only as one who is well versed but also as an enthusiast.

Thanks to these writers, and to many others besides, the enlightened part of the European public should have an adequate knowledge of Russia regarding multiple aspects of its current state. Yet, this knowledge of Russian things always leaves open a question of a different order, strongly obscured by powerful prejudices, and which, in Russia itself, has generally received only laughable solutions. Considered by many as an idle question and as too daring by others, this question is, in truth, the most important of all for a Russian, and, even aside from Russia, it cannot lack interest for the serious-minded. I mean the question of the *raison d'être* of Russia in regard to universal history.

When one sees this immense empire appear with more or less grandeur, after two centuries, on the scene of the world; when one sees it accept, on many secondary points, European civilization and yet reject it obstinately on others more important, thereby preserving an originality, which, albeit grounded in a negation, appears nevertheless imposing; when one sees this great historical *fact*, one asks: What, then, is the *thought* that hides or reveals it to us? What is the principal *ideal* that animates this powerful body? What new *word* will this newly arrived people say to humanity? What does it want to do in the history of the world? To resolve this question, we shall not address ourselves to the public opinion of today, which we run this risk of being disabused of tomorrow. We shall search for the response in eternal truths of religion. *For, the idea of a nation is not what it thinks of itself in time, but instead what God thinks of it in eternity.*

I

In accepting the essential and real unity of human-kind – and one rightly should accept it, because it is a religious truth justified by rational philosophy and confirmed by exact science – in accepting this substantial unity, we should consider the whole of humanity like a great collective being or a social organism of which different nations represent the living parts. It is evident, from this point of view, that no people would know how to live in itself, for itself, and by itself, but that the life of each people is nothing but a particular participation in the general life of humanity. The function that a nation should fulfill as being an organ[1] – that is its true national idea [*idée*], eternally fixed in the plan of God.

But, if it is true that humanity is a grand organism, it is still necessary to realize that it is not an organism that is purely physical, but that the members and elements of which it is composed – nations and individuals – are moral

---

1   Please see the Introduction for comments on the word *orga-nique*, a key word in this essay.

beings. Now, the essential condition of a moral being is that the particular function which it is called to fulfill in the life of the whole, the idea that determines its existence in the thought of God, is never imposed as a material necessity, but only as a moral obligation. God's thought, which is an absolute fatalism for [non-rational] things, is only a duty for a moral being. But if it is evident that a duty can be fulfilled or not; can be fulfilled well or badly; can be accepted or rejected; still, one would not know how to admit, on the other hand, that this liberty could change the providential plan or take away the efficacy of the moral law. The moral action of God cannot be less powerful than His physical action. It is necessary, therefore, to recognize that, in the moral world, there is also a fatalism, but a fatalism that is indirect and conditional. The vocation or the proper idea that God's thought assigns to each moral being – individual or nation – and what is revealed to the conscience of that being as its supreme duty — this is the idea that acts, in every case, like a real power; it determines, *in every case*, the existence of the moral being – but it does so in two opposed ways: it manifests itself as the Law of Life, when the duty is fulfilled, and as the Law of Death, when it is not. A moral being cannot ever escape the divine idea, which is its reason for being, but it depends upon itself to carry it in its heart and in its destiny as a blessing or as a curse.

What I have just said is or should be a commonplace for every – I will not say "Christian" – but for every monotheist. And, in fact, one finds nothing which must be put differently in these thoughts when they are presented in a general way; it is against their application to the question of nations that one protests. The commonplace is then transformed, all of a sudden, into a mystical dream, and the axiom becomes a subjective fantasy. "Who has ever known the thought of God about a nation, who could speak of the duty of a people? To affirm its power, to pursue its national interest: this is all that a people should do, and the duty of a patriot is reduced to supporting and serving his country in this national policy without imposing his own subjective ideas on it. And to know the real interests of a nation and its true mission in history, there is only one certain means, and that is to ask the people itself what it thinks about it; that is, to consult public opinion." There is, even so, something strange in this judgment which appears to be so sensible.

This empirical method to get at the truth is absolutely impracticable where national opinion is divided, which is almost always the case. What is the true opinion of the public of France: That of the Catholics, or that instead of the Freemasons? And since I myself am Russian: To which of the national opinions should I sacrifice my own subjective ideas, to that of official and officious Russia, *the Russia of today*; or instead to that which many millions of our Old Believers[2] profess, these true representatives of traditional

---

2 Also called *Razkolniki*, "breakaways," because they rejected the liturgical changes of the 17th century. The Old Believers still exist.

Russia, *the Russia of the past*, for whom our current church and state are the empire of the Antichrist; or, for that matter, should we deliver ourselves over to the Nihilists, who possibly represent *the future of Russia*?

II

I DO NOT NEED to press on about these difficulties, since history provides for the support of my thesis a proof that is immediate and known to everyone. If there is any truth attained by the philosophy of history, it is this: The definitive vocation of the Jewish people, its real reason for being, is fundamentally, essentially attached to the idea of the Messiah, that is to say, to the idea of the Christ.[3] It does not appear, however, that public opinion, the national sentiment of the Jews, has been very favorable to Christianity. I do not wish to address the usual reproaches made against this unique and mysterious people, which is, after all, the people of Prophets and Apostles, the people of Jesus Christ and the Blessed Virgin. This people lives even yet and the word of the New Testament promises to them a complete regeneration: "All of Israel will be saved" (Rom. 11:26). And – I have to say this, even though

---

3 *Meshiakh* (Messiah) in Hebrew is *Christos* in Greek.

I cannot prove here this assertion[4] – the "hardening"[5] of the Jews is not the only cause of their hostile position in regard to Christianity. In Russia above all, where one has never attempted to apply the principles of Christianity to the Jews, shall we dare to demand of them to be more Christian than ourselves?

I have wished only to recall this remarkable historical fact: That the people called to give Christianity to the world has accomplished this mission only in spite of itself; that it persists, for the greatest part, and for eighteen centuries, in rejecting the divine idea which it had carried in its bosom and which has been its true reason for being. We can therefore dismiss henceforth the notion that the popular opinion of a nation is always right and that a people can never misunderstand or refuse its true calling.

But possibly this historical fact which I invoke is nothing more than a religious prejudice, and the fatal link that is proposed between the Chosen People of Israel and Christianity is nothing but a subjective fantasy on my part. I can, however, produce an extremely simple proof which makes evident the real and objective character of the fact in question.

If one takes our Christian Bible, the collection of books which begins with Genesis and finishes with the Apocalypse,

---

4   (1) I have attempted to do so in two studies in regard to the Jews, of which the first was analyzed in the *Revue française*, September and October, 1886.

5   Cf. Acts 19:8-9

and if one examines it outside of any religious conviction, as a simple historical and literarary monument, one is forced to affirm that there is a complete and harmonious work here: The creation of heaven and of the earth and the fall of humanity in the first Adam, at the beginning; the restoration of humanity in the second Adam or Christ at the center; and, at the end, the apocalyptic apotheosis, the creation of a new heaven and a new earth where where justice reigns, the revelation of a world transfigured and glorified, the new Jerusalem descending from the heavens, the tabernacle where God lives with men (Rev. 21). The end of the work attaches itself here to the beginning; the creation of the physical world and the history of humanity are explained and justified by the revelation of the spiritual world which is the perfect union of humanity with God. The work is finished, the circle is closed, and even from a purely aesthetic point of view one is satisfied. Let us look now how the Bible of the Hebrews finishes. The last book of this Bible is *Divrei-ha-yamim*, Chronicles, and here is the conclusion of the last chapter:

> Cyrus, king of Persia, said thus: "All the kingdoms of the earth have been given to me by Yahweh, God of the Heavens; and He ordered me to build for Him a house in Jerusalem which is in Judea. Who among you here is from all His people? May Yahweh, his God, be with him and let him come up."[6]

---

6   II Chr. 36:23.

Between this ending and that of the Christian Bible; between the words of Christ glorified, "I am the Alpha and the Omega, the beginning and the end; I give freely to him who thirsts for the source of the living water; whoever is victorious will inherit everything, and I will be his God and he will be a son to Me"[7]; between these words and those of the king of Persia; between this house which he was to build in Jerusalem of Judea and the habitation of God with men in the new Jerusalem descending from the heavens, the contrast is really striking. From the point of view of the Jews who reject the great, universal fulfillment of their national history revealed in the New Testament, it would be necessary to admit that the creation of the heaven and the earth, the calling of the patriarchs, the mission of Moses, the miracles of Exodus, the revelation at Sinai, the exploits and hymns of David, the wisdom of Solomon, the inspiration of the Prophets – all these marvels and all these holy glories would not have attained anything in the end except a declaration from a pagan king ordering a handful of Jews to build the second Temple of Jerusalem, a temple of such poverty compared to the splendor of the first that it made the aged of Judea cry, and which afterwards was enlarged and embellished by Herod, an Idumean,[8] only to be destroyed definitively by the soldiers of Titus. This is not a subjective prejudice of a Christian, it is the monument of the national thought of the Hebrews themselves, which

---

7 Rev. 21:6-7.

8 A Gentile.

demonstrates manifestly that, without Christianity, the work of Israel in history has failed, and that, consequently, a people certainly can sometimes fall short of its vocation.

III

I HAVE NOT STRAYED off topic in speaking of the Bible of the Jews, for there is something in this truncated Bible, in this contrast of a grandiose beginning and a contemptible end; there is something which reminds me of the fortunes of Russia, if one envisions them from an exclusively nationalist point of view, which is dominant among us today and which unites in a tacit accord the Caiphas' and Herods of our bureaucracy with the zelots of militant pan-Slavism.

Truly, when I think of the prophetic rays of a great future which illumined the beginnings of our history; when I recall the noble and wise act of national abdication which, more than a thousand years ago, created the Russian State, when our ancestors, seeing the insufficiency of indigenous elements to organize the social order, willingly and deliberately called upon the foreign power of Scandinavian princes with a memorable phrase: "Our country is great and fertile, but there is no order in it. Come dominate and rule over us." And after an establishment of such originality of the material order, the introduction not less remarkable of Christianity, and the splendid figure of St. Vladimir, a fervent and fanatical servant of idols who, after having sensed both the inadequacy of paganism and the interior need of the true religion, reflected and deliberated for a long time before accepting it; but once he became a Christian, he wished to be so entirely, and not only did he give himself to works of charity in taking care of the poor and the sick, but he also showed himself more pen-etrated by the evangelical writings than the Greek bishops who baptized him; for these bishops succeeded only by the force of specious arguments to persuade this prince, previously prone to bloodshed, to inflict the death pen-alty on brigands and assassins. "I have fear of commit-ting sin," he would say to his spiritual fathers. And then, when to this "beautiful sun" – for so the popular poetry surnamed our first Christian prince – when to this beau-tiful sun which illumined the beginnings of our history succeeded centuries of darkness and troubles; when, after a long series of calamities, driven back into the cold forests of the Northeast, benumbed by enslavement and the ne-cessity of harsh work on a barren soil, separated from the civilized world, and barely accessible even to the ambas-sadors of the head of Christianity,[9] the Russian people fell into a state of coarse barbarity heightened by a national

9 (2) See the interesting study by Fr. Pierling, [S.J.], *Rome et Moscou*, 1547-1579.   [Available at https://archive.org/details/romeetmoscou00piergoog.]

pride that was both stupid and ignorant; when, forgetting the true Christianity of St. Vladimir, Moscovite piety relentlessly pursued absurd disputes about details of ritual; and when thousands of men were sent to the bonfire for having held too much to certain typographical errors in the old church books;[10] suddenly, from this chaos of barbarism and miseries, arises the colossal and unique figure of Peter the Great. Rejecting the blind Moscovite nationalism, penetrated by an enlightened patriotism which saw the true needs of his country, he stopped at nothing to impose on Russia the civilization which he despised but which he considered necessary for it. He not only called in that foreign civilization as a powerful protector, but he also found himself in his station to be its humble servant and diligent apprentice, and despite the great defects of his private character, he provided to the end an admirable example of devotion to duty and civic virtue. Very well! In recalling all this one may say to himself: The definitive national work that had such precursors must therefore be quite grand and beautiful; the country must aim very high, if it does not wish to decline, which even in its barbarian state was represented by St. Vladimir and Peter the Great. But the true grandeurs of Russia are a dead letter for our so-called patriots who wish to impose upon the Russian people a historical mission suited to their own fashion and their own capabilities. Our national work would be, according to their way of thinking, the simplest thing in

---

10 The Old Believers.

the world: Russia would have but one force, the force of arms. To give the *coup de grâce* to the Ottoman Empire which is expiring, and then to destroy the monarchy of the Hapsburgs, and to put into the place of these two powers a mass of petty independent national kingdoms which would only await the solemn hour of their definitive emancipation in order to rush upon one another. So that is what Russia had to suffer and fight for for a thousand years, to become Christian with St. Vladimir and European with Peter the Great, always maintaining a place apart from the Orient and the West – all that to become definitively an instrument for Greater Serbia and Greater Bulgaria!

But, one will tell us, that is not really the point: The real end of our national politics is Constantinople. To all appearance, one no longer takes into account the Greeks who themselves have, nevertheless, a notion of "Greater Greece." But the most important thing is to know: With what, and in the name of what, can we enter Constantinople? What can we bring there other than the pagan idea of the absolute State, the principles of Caesaropapism which we have borrowed from the Greeks and who have already lost the Lower Empire? In universal history there are mysterious events, but there are none that are absurd. No! This is not the Russia that we see, a Russia unfaithful to its thousands of memories, to the lessons of Vladimir and Peter the Great, a Russia possessed by a blind nationalism and a wild obscurantism; it is not she who could ever seize the second Rome and terminate the fatal question of the East.

If, through our fault, this question cannot be resolved to our greater glory, it will be to our greater humiliation. If Russia persists on the path of oppressive obscurantism she has just entered, she will be replaced in the East by another national force less endowed but all the more consistent even in its inferiority. The Bulgarians, our beloved protégés of yesterday, our rebels so much looked down upon today, will be, tomorrow, our triumphant rivals and the masters of old Byzantium.

IV

YET, IT IS not necessary to exaggerate these pessimistic apprehensions. Russia has not yet abdicated its reason for being, it has not denied the faith and the love of its earliest youth. She remains free to renounce this politics of egoism and national stupidity which would make it necessary for us to abandon our mission in history. The misleading product which one calls "public opinion," manufactured and sold cheaply by an opportunistic press, has not yet suffocated our national consciousness which will know how to find a more authentic expression of the true idea of Russia. It is not necessary to go far for it: it is quite close. The true idea of Russia, attested by the religious character of the people, is prefigured and indicated by the most important events and the greatest personages of our history. And if that is not sufficient, there is a testimony yet greater and more certain: the revealed word of God. Not that this word has ever said anything about Russia: it is its silence, on the contrary, which shows us the true way. If the only people about which divine Providence is specifically concerned is the People of Israel; if the reason for being of this unique people was not in itself, but rather in the Christian revelation which it prepared the way for; and if, finally, in the New Testament there is no longer a question of any nationality in particular, and it is even expressly declared that no national antagonisms ought to exist any longer; should one therefore not conclude that in the primordial thought of God, nations do not exist apart from their organic and living unity – that is, apart from humanity? And if this is so in regard to God, it should also be so for the nations themselves, insofar as they wish to realize their true identity, which is nothing other than their manner of being in the eternal thought of God.

The reason for being of nations is not found in themselves but in humanity. But where is this humanity? Is it not merely a construct of reason[11] that does not have any real existence? It would be just as true to say that the arm and the leg exist but that a whole man is nothing but a construct of reason. Besides, all zoologists know of animals (for the most part pertaining to the lower class called *actinozoa*, e.g., jellyfish, polyps, etc.) which are only, fundamentally, highly differentiated organs leading an isolated life, in such a way that the complete animal exists only as an idea.[12] Such also was the manner of being of humankind before Christianity, when there was nothing in reality but

---

11 *être de raison*. In Latin, *ens rationis*, something that exists only in the imagination or intellect, not extramentally.

12 The term *actinozoa* is now obsolete.

the *disjecta membra* – separated limbs – of the all-embracing man, tribes and nations separated or partially reunited by an external force, when the true essential unity of humanity was nothing but a promise, a prophetic idea. But this idea *assumed a body* at the moment when, in Christ, the absolute center of all beings was revealed. From that time, the great unity of mankind, the all-embracing body of the God-Man, really existed upon the Earth. It is not perfect, but it exists; it is not perfect, but it advances toward perfection, it grows and extends externally and develops internally. Humanity is no longer a mere construct of reason: its substantial form comes into actuality in Christianity, in the universal Church.[13]

For each people to participate in the life of the universal Church, in the development of the great Christian civilization, and to participate according to the particular forces and capacities given to it: This is the only true aim, the only true mission of every people. It is an evident and elementary truth that the role [*idée*] of a particular organ cannot be isolated and put into antagonism with the other organs, but instead is the reason for its unity and solidarity with all the parts of the living body. And, from the Christian point of view, one would not know how to object to the application of this truth, which is quite elementary, to integral humanity which is the living body of Christ. It is for this reason that Christ Himself, in the very act of

---

13   The Greek word for "universal" is *katholike*, from which the word "Catholic" derives.

recognizing, in His definitive[14] word to the Apostles, the existence and vocation of *all the nations* (Matt. 23:19) nevertheless did not draw attention to it, nor did He direct His disciples to any nation in particular: This is because, for Him, they did not exist except for their organic and moral union as living members of one and only one spiritual and real body. And so Christian truth affirms the permanent existence of *nations* and the rights of *nationality*, all the while condemning *nationalism*, which is, for a people, what egoism is for an individual: The evil principle which tends to isolate distinct beings by transforming difference into division and division into antagonism.

---

14   *première*, indicating the level of importance rather than the order of time, as the biblical reference is near the very end of St. Matthew's Gospel.

V

THE RUSSIAN PEOPLE is a Christian people, and consequently, to know the true idea of Russia it is not necessary to ask what Russia will do by herself and for herself, but what she *should do* in the name of the Christian principle which she recognizes, and for the good of the whole of Christianity to which she is reckoned to belong. She should, in order to fulfill her mission truly, enter with heart and soul into the common life of the Christian world and employ all her national forces to bring about, cooperatively with the other peoples, this perfect and universal unity of humankind, of which the immutable base is given to us in the Church of Christ. But the spirit of national egoism does not allow itself to be sacrificed so easily. It has found among us a means of affirming itself without openly denying the inherent religious character of the Russian nationality. One not only admits that the Russian people is a Christian people, but one also proclaims with emphasis that it is the Christian people *par excellence* and that the Church is the true base of our national life; but this is only by pretending that *the Church is among only us*, that we have a monopoly on Christian life and faith. In this way, the Church which is, in reality, the unbreakable rock of universal unity and solidarity becomes, for Russia, a palladium of a closed-in national particularism, and often even the passive instrument of a politics that is egotistic and hateful.

Our religion, so far as it is manifested in the faith of the people and in the Divine Liturgy, is perfectly orthodox. The Russian Church, insofar as it conserves the truth of the Faith, the perpetuity of apostolic succession, and the validity of the Sacraments, participates, in its essence, in the unity of the universal Church founded by Christ. And if, sadly, this unity exists among us only in a latent state and does not come to be a living reality, it is because certain secular chains keep the body of our Church attached to an unclean corpse which suffocates it while decomposing.

The official institution which is represented by our ecclesiastical government, and by our theological school, and which maintains, at any cost, its particularist and exclusive character, is certainly *not* a living part of the true, universal Church founded by Christ. To say what it is in reality, we leave the word to an author whose testimony at this occasion has exceptional value. One of the most eminent leaders of the "Russian party," an ardent patriot and zealous Orthodox, in his capacity as a Slavophile and declared enemy of the West in general and the Church of Rome in particular, regarding the papacy with horror and the Company of Jesus[15] as an abomination, I. S. Aksakov[16] could not be suspected of having any preconceived ideas that are unfavorable to our national Church as such. On the other hand, even though he may share in the prejudices and errors of his party, Aksakov has risen above the level of vulgar Panslavists not only by his talent, but also by his good faith, by the sincerity of his thought and the frankness of his speech. Persecuted by the administration for a long time, condemned finally to silence for twelve years, it was only in the last years of his life that he obtained, as a personal privilege, and always a precarious one at that, the relative freedom to publish what he thought.

---

15 The Society of Jesus, the Jesuits.
16 Ivan Sergeyevich Aksakov, 1823-86.

VI

L ET US HEAR, then, this trustworthy and quite well au-
thorized witness. He supported his judgment on a
long series of incontestable facts which we must omit here;
his word by itself will suffice for us.

> Our Church, from the standpoint of its govern-
> ment, appears as a kind of colossal bureau or sec-
> retariat which applies to the office of pastoring
> the flock of Christ all the procedures of German
> bureaucracy, with all the official falsity which is
> inherent to them.[17] The ecclesiastical govern-
> ment has been organized like a lay department of
> administration; and the ministers of the Church
> having been counted as government workers,[18]
> the Church herself has been transformed there-
> upon into a function of the secular power; or, to

---

17   (3) *Complete Works of Ivan Aksakov*, vol. 4, p. 124. [Available
     at https://archive.org/details/sochineniiaisaks04aksa.]

18   *serviteurs de l'État*, servants of the State.

put it quite simply, she enters into the service of the State. In appearance one has done nothing more than introduce the necessary order into the Church, but it is her soul that one has taken away from her. For the ideal of a government that is truly spiritual, one has substituted that of an order purely formal and exterior. It is not a question here only of secular power, but above all of *secular ideas* that have entered into our ecclesiastical milieu and have taken hold of the soul and spirit of our clergy to such an extent that the mission of the Church in the true and living sense has become barely comprehensible.[19] We have certain "enlightened" ecclesiastics who propose that our religious life has not been sufficiently regulated by the State, and they ask of the State a new code of laws and regulations for the Church. And yet, in the current code of the Empire,[20] one finds more than a thousand articles determining the guardianship of the State over the Church and detailing the functions of the police in the domain of faith and piety.

The secular government is declared by our code "the conserver of dogmas of the dominant faith and the guardian of good order in the holy

---

19 (4) *Ibid.* pp. 125, 126.
20 Under the Czars at the time of the writing, 1888.

Church." We see this guardian, with sword raised, ready to strike down on any infraction of this orthodoxy, established less with the assistance of the Holy Spirit than with that of the penal laws of the Russian Empire.[21] *"Where there is no living and internal unity, external union [intégrité] can only be sustained by violence and fraud."*[22]

In regard to the cruel persecution brought about by the ecclesiastical and civil government against an indigenous sect of Protestants (the Shtundists) in southern Russia, Aksakov gives a vigorous expression to his righteous indignation:

> To suppress by imprisonment spiritual thirst *when there is nothing to satisfy it*; to resort to prison as an answer to the sincere need of faith and to the questions of religious thought that are awakened; to prove, by imprisonment, the truth of Orthodoxy; that is to undermine all the basis of our religion and surrender one's arms to victorious Protestantism.[23]

And yet it is found that these penal laws, with their "imprisonment," which has so disgraced our country, are absolutely indispensable to conserve "the dominant Church." The defenders of this Church who are the most sincere

---

21 (5) *Ibid*. p. 84.
22 (6) *Ibid*. p. 100.
23 (7) *Ibid*. p. 72.

and reasonable (for example, Pogodine, cited along with many others by our author) openly avow that religious liberty, once admitted into Russia, would mean that half of the Orthodox peasants would pass over to *raskol* (the schism of the Old Believers which is quite numerous in spite of all the persecutions of them) and the other half of the people would become Catholic.

> What does an admission like this mean? Aksasov inquires;[24] that half of the members of the Orthodox Church belong to it only in appearance, that these men are kept in her bosom only by fear of temporal punishments. And that is thus the current state of our Church! A state of being unworthy, distressing, and frightful! What a superabundance of sacrileges within the holy enclosure, of hypocrisy which takes the place of truth, of terror in place of love, of corruption under the outward appearance of order, of false faith in violent opposition to true faith; what negation, within the Church itself, of the vital principles of the Church, of all her reason for being; deceit and incredulity, precisely where everything should live, move, and have its being by truth and faith... And yet the gravest danger is not the evil which has penetrated into the midst of the believers, but that which has received *rights of*

---

24 Solovyov has apparently inserted the words "Aksakov inquires" into this quotation from him.

citizenship, namely, that this position of the Church has been created by the law, that an anomaly like this is merely a necessary consequence of the way things are ruled by the State and by our society itself.[25]

In general, among us in Russia, in Church matters as in others, it is the appearance, the decorum, which one must adhere to above all, and that suffices for our love for the Church, for our slothful love, for our slack faith. We gladly close our eyes and, in our puerile fear of scandal, we force ourselves to hide from ourselves and likewise from the whole world the great evil that, beneath a respectable veil, devours the vital substance of our religious organism like a cancer.[26]

There is nowhere else where truth is so held in horror than in the domain of our ecclesiastical government, nowhere else where servility is greater than in our spiritual hierarchy, nowhere else where "the salutary lie" is applied at a greater scale than precisely where every lie should be abhorred. There is nowhere else where one allows, under the pretext of prudence, so much compromise that diminishes the Church and takes away her authority.

---

25 (8) *Ibid.* p. 91.
26 (9) *Ibid.* p. 42.

And the principal cause of all this is that one does not have enough faith in the power of the truth.[27]

All of these evils of our Church – and this is the most important point – we have known and currently know; we make ourselves get along with them and we live in peace. But this shameful peace, these disgraceful compromises, cannot safeguard the peace of the Church, and in the cause of truth they signify a defeat if not a betrayal.[28]

If one must believe its defenders, our Church is a large but unfaithful flock, of which the pastor is the policeman who, by force, by strike of the lash, makes the wayward sheep enter into fold. Does an image like this really correspond to the true idea of the Church of Christ? And if not, then our Church is no longer the Church of Christ, and so what is it, then? An institution of the State that could be useful to the State interest in the control [*discipline*] of morals. But the Church, it must not be forgotten, is a domain where no alteration of the basis of morality can be admitted; where no infidelity to the vivifying principle can remain unpunished; where, if one lies, one is lying not to men but to God. A Church unfaithful to the testament of Christ is, of

---

27 (10) *Ibid.* p. 32.
28 (11) *Ibid.* p. 43.

all the things in the world, the most sterile and ab-
normal phenomenon condemned in advance by the
word of God.[29]

A Church that becomes part of a State, of a "kingdom of this world," has abdicated its mission and
should partake of the destiny of all the kingdoms of
this world.[30] It no longer has any reason for being; it
condemns itself to weakness and death.[31]

The Russian conscience is not free in Russia, and
religious thought remains inert; the abomination
of desolation establishes itself in the holy place; the
breath of death replaces the spirit that gives life;
the spiritual sword – the word – is covered with
rust, supplanted by the material sword of the State;
and near to the doors of the Church, instead of
angels of God watching over its entrances and ex-
its, one sees military police[32] and police inspectors:
these are the guardians of orthodox dogmas, these
are the [spiritual] directors of our conscience.[33]

29 (12) *Ibid.* p. 91, 92.
30 (13) *Ibid.* p. 111.
31 (14) *Ibid.* p. 93.
32 *gendarmes.*
33 (15) *Ibid.* p. 83, 84.

And here, in a word, the final conclusion of this rigorous examination:

> The spirit of truth, the spirit of charity, the spirit of life, the spirit of liberty – it is their gentle and salutary breath that is missing in the Russian Church.[34]

---

34 (16) *Ibid.* p. 127.

VII

AN INSTITUTION WHICH the Spirit of truth has abandoned cannot possibly be the true Church of God. To recognize it, it is not necessary to abdicate the religion of our fathers; it is not necessary to renounce the piety of the Orthodox people, their sacred traditions, and all the holy things which they venerate. It is evident, on the contrary, that the only thing we must sacrifice to the truth is the pseudo-ecclesiastical establishment characterized so well by that Orthodox writer above – this establishment which has servility and material interest for its base, and fraud and violence for its means of action.

The system of governmental materialism which rested exclusively on the brutal force of arms and regarded as nothing the moral strength of free thought and speech – this materialistic system brought us once to the disasters of Sebastopol.[35] The conscience of the Russian people faithfully represented by its sovereign spoke in a loud voice. Russia made an act of penitence and revealed itself by an

---

35 1854-55, during the Crimean War.

act of justice, the emancipation of the serfs.[36] This act, which was the glory of a great reign, is, even so, only a beginning. The work of social emancipation cannot content itself with remaining on the material level. The body of Russia is free, but the national spirit is still waiting for its Feb. 19th. It is, therefore, not with the body alone, it is not with an endeavor that is purely material, that Russia can accomplish its mission in history and manifest its true national identity [idée]. And how could it manifest itself, this poor Russian identity, confined into a narrow prison, deprived of air and light, and guarded by evil and jealous eunuchs?

It is not by retreating to the reign of Nicholas I[37] and imitating the grand errors of this grand sovereign that one could repair the essential faults in the incomplete work of Alexander II.[38] One should not tempt Providence in forgetting too quickly the historical lessons it has given us. It is allowed to hope that the religious sentiment, good will, and right reason which distinguish the current emperor[39] will know how to defend him against ill-inspired counselors who would want to impose on him the unspeakable policy judged and condemned at Sebastopol.

The religious and intellectual emancipation of Russia is an act which imposes itself today upon our government

---

36 Feb. 19, 1861 (Old Style calendar).
37 Reigned 1825-55.
38 Reigned 1855-81.
39 Alexander III, reigned 1881-94.

with as much necessity as the emancipation of the serfs imposed itself thirty years ago during the government of Alexander II. Serfdom was likewise useful and necessary at one time in the past. In the same way, the official guardianship imposed upon the national spirit of Russia was able to be beneficial when this spirit was in its infancy; today, it can only suffocate it. It is useless to repeat unceasingly that our national organism is full of health and vigor, as if it were strictly necessary for it to be weak and feeble for it to be suffocated. Whatever may be the intrinsic qualities of the Russian people, they cannot operate in a normal manner while their conscience and thought remain paralyzed by a regime of violence and obscurantism. We must,[40] above all, give free access to pure air and light; remove artificial barriers that keep the religious spirit of our nation in a state of isolation and inertia; we must open for it a direct road towards the complete and living truth.

But one has fear of the truth because the truth is catholic, that is to say, universal. One wants to have, at any price, a separate religion, an Imperial Church. One does not hold it for oneself, but one wants to keep it as an attribute and as a sanction of an exclusivist nationalism. But those who will not sacrifice their national egoism to universal truth cannot and should not call themselves Christians.

---

40 *Il s'agit de.* This could also mean "It is a matter of" taking the measures stated.

Our people are now preparing to celebrate solemnly the ninth centennial of Christianity in Russia. But it seems that that would be a premature festivity. To listen to certain patriots, the baptism of St. Vladimir, so efficacious for the prince himself, has not been for his nation more than a baptism of water, and it is still necessary for us to be baptized a second time by the spirit of truth and the fire of charity. And truly this second baptism is absolutely necessary, if not for the whole of Russia, at least for the part of our society that acts and speaks today. To become Christian, it should renounce a new idolatry that is less crass but not less absurd, and much more pernicious than the idolatry of our pagan ancestors, rejected by St. Vladimir. I mean this new idolatry, this epidemic folly of nationalism which drives people to adore their own image in place of the supreme and universal Divinity.

VIII

To MAINTAIN AND manifest the Christian character of Russia, it is necessary for us to abdicate definitively the false divinity of the age, and to sacrifice to the true God our national egoism. Providence has put us in a particular condition which should render this sacrifice more complete and more efficacious. There is an elementary moral law which is imposed equally on individuals and on nations, and which is expressed in this word of the Gospel, which commands us, before sacrificing on the altar, to make peace with the brother who has anything against us. The Russian people has a brother who has certain profound grievances against it, and it behooves us to make peace with this people which is both a brother and an enemy, in order to begin the sacrifice of our national egoism upon the altar of the Universal Church.

This is not a matter of sentiment, although sentiment should also have its place in human relations. But between a sentimental politics [*politique*] and a politics of egoism and violence, there is a middle term: the politics of moral obligation and justice. I do not wish to examine here the pretensions of the Poles regarding the restoration of their ancient kingdom, nor the objections which the Russians could bring forth against it in their turn. It is not a question of problematic plans to be realized, but of a manifest and incontestable iniquity which we must renounce in any case. I mean the odious system of Russification, which has nothing to do with political autonomy, but which attacks the national existence, even the very soul, of the Polish people. To Russify Poland, or in other words, to kill a nation that has a very well developed self-consciousness, which has a glorious history and which has surpassed us in its intellectual culture, and which, even today, does not take second place to us in scientific or literary activity. And although in these conditions the definitive aim of our Russifiers is, fortunately, impossible to attain, yet everything one undertakes to arrive at that is nonetheless criminal and detrimental. This tyrannical Russification, intimately connected with destruction, still more tyrannical, of the Uniate Greek Church,[41] is a real national sin, which weighs on the conscience of Russia and paralyzes its moral forces.

One has seen some great nations triumph over a long period of time in an unjust cause. But it seems that Providence, by a particular solicitude for the salvation of our national soul, hastens to show us, with perfect

---

41　A church Eastern (specifically, Greek) in its rite but fully united to and under the See of Peter.

evidence, that force, even when victorious, is not good for
anyone when it is not directed by a pure conscience. Our
historic sin has taken away from our last war its practical
results and its moral value at the same time; it pursues, in
the Balkans, our victorious eagles and stops them before
the walks of Constantinople; in taking away from us the
assurance and spiritedness of a people faithful to its mission, this sin imposes upon us, in lieu of a triumph pur-
chased by so many heroic efforts, the humiliation of the
Congress of Berlin;[42] and it ends up driving us out of Serbia
and Bulgaria, which we would want to protect, while at the
same time oppressing Poland.

This oppressive system, which is not applied to Poland
alone, thoroughly evil as it is in itself, becomes all the worse
by flagrant contradiction, where it is found alongside gen-
erous ideas of emancipation and disinterested protection,
which Russian politics has always claimed for itself. This
policy is necessarily permeated with falsity and hypocrisy,
which take away all prestige from it and render impossible
every lasting success. One cannot inscribe with impuni-
ty upon one's standard the liberty of enslaved and other
peoples, all the while taking away the national liberty of
the Polish, the religious liberty of the Uniates and Russian
dissidents, and the civil rights of the Jews.

It is not in this sort of state – with a shut mouth, the
eyes blindfolded, and the soul torn apart by contradictions

---

42   1878, in which Germany, under Bismarck, accomplished
humiliating measures against Russia.

and remorse – that Russia should enter into her work in history. We have already had two profound lessons, two severe warnings: at Sebastopol, first, and then, in circumstances even more significant, Berlin. We must not wait for yet a third warning, which could be, perhaps, the last. To repent of her historic sins and satisfy justice; to abdicate national egoism by renouncing the policy of Russification and by allowing, without reservation, religious liberty – that is the only way, for Russia, to prepare herself for the revelation and the realization of her true national identity which – one must not forget – is not an abstract idea nor a blind fatality, but above all a moral obligation. The idea of Russia – Russian identity – as we know, cannot be anything other than a determined aspect of Christian identity, and the mission of our people can be clear to us only in so far as we enter into the true sense of Christianity.

IX

IT WAS JUST about thirty or forty years ago that certain writers, more or less respectable, preached to us,
in France as well as in Russia,[43] an ideal Christianity and
Church, the spiritual Kingdom of free brotherhood and
perfect love. That is, without doubt, the ideal, that is to
say, the future of the Church. The teaching of these au-
thors is a prophecy. But in not being a *false* prophecy, it
should indicate to us the direct way and the good means
to realize this absolute ideal. An ideal, if it is not an empty
dream, cannot be anything other than the realizable perfection of what is given. Would it be in renouncing the
past of the universal Church and in destroying its current
form that one would arrive at the ideal reign of fraternity

---

43 (17) In regard to France, I mean what Mr. Anatole Leroy-
Beaulieu has called so well, "the obscure and powerless school
of Bordat-Dumoulin and Huet." (See *Les catholiques libéraux*, p.
182). In Russia, the ideas of Bordat-Dumoulin have been ad-
opted by Khomiakoff, who employed his considerable talent in
popularizing these ideas by giving them a false air of Greco-
Russian Orthodoxy.

and perfect love? That would only be the application, very badly placed, of a parricide law which governs our mortal life. In this life, determined by the state of corrupted nature, a new generation arrives at the pleasure of the present only by ignobly supplanting its ancestors, but it is for this reason, too, that this criminal existence lasts only for a moment; and if Chronos, after having mutilated and supplanted the old Uranos, was himself suppressed by Zeus, whom he was not able to swallow, this new god himself ascended to the sullied throne only to undergo, in turn, a similar destiny. Such is the law of life that is falsified and corrupted, of a life that should not be, seeing that it is more dead than alive, and that is why humanity, fatigued by this infinite misery, awaited with anguish as its true savior *a Son of God Who was not the rival of His Father.* And now that this true Son Who does not replace, but Who manifests and glorifies His Father, has come and has given a law of immortal life to all of regenerated humanity, to the universal Church, one still aspires to introduce, under a different guise, in this Church itself, in this organism and true life, the abolished law of death!

In truth, in the universal Church, the past and the future, the tradition and the ideal, far from being mutually exclusive, are equally essential and indispensable to constitute the true present of humanity, its well-being here and now. Piety, justice, and charity, strangers to every envy and every rivalry, should form a permanent and indissoluble bond among the three principal agents of social and historic humanity; among the representatives of its past unity, its present multiplicity, and its future totality.

The principle of the past or of *paternity* is realized in the Church by the *priesthood*, spiritual fathers, the elders or ancients *par excellence* (priest, from *presbyteros* = elder), representing on Earth the heavenly Father, the Ancient of Days. And for the general or catholic Church, there should exist a general or international priesthood, centralized and unified in the person of a common Father for all peoples, the universal Pontiff. It is evident, in fact, that a national priesthood cannot represent as such the general paternity which should equally embrace all nations. As regards the reunion of different national clergies into a sole ecumenical body, this cannot be effected but by an international center, real and permanent, capable as a matter of right and of fact of resisting all particularist tendencies.

The real unity of a family cannot subsist in a regular and durable manner without a common father or someone who takes his place. To turn individuals and people into a family, a real fraternity, the paternal principle of religion should be a reality here below in an ecclesiastical monarchy that can effectively reunite around itself all national and individual elements, and always serve for them as a living image and a free instrument of celestial fatherhood.

The universal or international priesthood with the Supreme Pontiff as a unique center reproduces, in spiritualizing it, the primitive age of humanity, when all peoples were really united by common origin and by the identity of their religious ideas and the rules of life. That is the rule of life *of the past* of humankind, the past which does not weigh heavily on the present but which serves as immutable base for it, and which does not exclude the future, yet is essentially one with it. As regards the *present* of humanity, we see it determined by the diversity of nations which have a tendency to constitute themselves into *complete bodies* or States each having a particular independent center, a secular power or temporal government that represents and directs the combined action of national forces. The interests of the whole of humanity do not exist for the State and for the secular government, whose duties are limited to that fraction of humankind it is in charge of. The universal Church, while guarding by means of its sacerdotal order united under the Sovereign Pontiff, the religion of the common paternity, the great, eternal past of our species, does not exclude, even so, the present diversity of nations and of States. The only thing the Church can never sanction, and in that she is the faithful organ of the truth and of the will of God, is divisions and national rivalries as a definitive condition of human society. The true Church will always condemn the doctrine that affirms that there is nothing beyond national interests, this new paganism which makes a nation its supreme deity, this false patriotism which wishes to replace religion. The Church, in combatting national egoism, recognizes the rights of nations; she respects the power of the State in resisting the absolutism thereof.

National differences are bound to exist to the end of the ages; peoples are bound to remain as truly distinct members of the universal organism. But this organism itself should truly exist as well; the grand unity of humanity should not exist only as a hidden force or as only a concept of reason but should be incarnated in a social, visible body exercising an action attractive, manifest, and permanent to put in check the multitude of centrifugal forces that tear humanity apart.

To attain the ideal of perfect unity it is necessary to rely upon an *imperfect* unity, but yet *real*. Before reuniting in liberty, it is necessary to reunite in obedience. To arrive at universal *fraternity*, nations, states, and sovereigns need to submit first to universal *filiation* in recognizing the moral authority of the common father. The forgetfulness of sentiments which peoples owe to the religious past of humanity must be a very evil portent for its future. When one sows impiety, it is not fraternity that one reaps.

The real future of humanity, for which we ought to work, is *universal fraternity proceeding from universal paternity though a permanent moral and social filiation.* This future, which, to make a complete ideal a reality, should bring into accord the interests of current-day life with the rights of the past, has been at all times represented in the Church of God through *true prophets.* The society of God with men, or the universal Church (in the broad sense of the word), having in the priesthood the organ of its fundamental religious unity and in temporal power the organ of its current national pluralism, should manifest in this way its absolute *totality*, its unity both free and perfect through the instrument of prophets spontaneously brought forth by the spirit of God to bring light to peoples and their leaders in maintaining before them the *complete* ideal of human society.

X

THUS, THE THREE terms of social existence are found *simultaneously* represented in the true life of the universal Church, directed in turn by these three principal agents: the spiritual authority, or the universal Pontiff (infallible head of the priesthood), representing the permanent, true past of humanity; the secular power of the national sovereign (legitimate head of the State), concentrating in himself and personifying the interests, rights, and duties of the present; and finally the free ministry of the prophet (inspired head of human society in its totality) inaugurating the realization of the ideal future of humanity. The harmonious concord and action of these three principal factors are the first condition of true progress. The Supreme Pontiff is the representative of the true eternal paternity and not of false paternity, namely, that of Chronos (Time) of the pagans who devoured his own children. He [the Supreme Pontiff], instead, finds his life only in their life. While faithfully keeping and affirming the immutable unity of tradition, the Universal Pontiff is under obligation to exclude neither the legitimate interests of the present, nor the noble aspirations for a perfect ideal; to preserve the past well, he does not have to bind the present and close the door to the future. For his part, the head of the national State, if he is worthy of his power, should think and act as a true son of the Universal Church (represented by the Sovereign Pontiff), and then he is the image and a veritable organ of the Son and of the eternal King, of Him Who does the will of His Father and not His own, and Who does not wish to be glorified except in glorifying His Father. Finally, the free initiator of progressive social movement, the prophet, if he does not betray his great vocation, if he puts his individual inspiration in accord with the universal tradition and his liberty – the true liberty of the sons of God – in accord with filial piety in regard to the sacred authority and with the proper respect towards legitimate powers and duties, becomes a veritable organ of the Holy Spirit Who has spoken through the Prophets and Who animates the universal Body of Christ in making it aspire to absolute perfection. More complete is the simultaneous union of these three representatives of the past, the present, and the future of humanity; more decisive is the victory of the universal Church over the fatal law of time and of death; more intimate is the bond which attaches our earthly existence to the eternal life of the divine Trinity.

As in the Trinity, in which each of the three hypostases is perfectly God and, therefore, *in virtue of their consubstantiality*, there is only one God, each of the three Persons not having a separate existence and never finding itself outside substantial and indivisible unity with the other two; in the same way each of the three principal dignitaries of the theocratic society possesses a veritable sovereignty, yet without there being, even so, three different absolute powers in the universal Church or in one of its parts, because the three representatives of the divino-human sovereignty should be *in absolute solidarity* among themselves, merely forming three principal organs of one and the same social body, exercising three fundamental functions of one and the same collective life.

In the divine Trinity, the third Person presupposes the first two in their unity.[44] So should it be in the social Trinity of humanity. The free and perfect organization of society, which is the mission of the true prophets, supposes the union and solidarity of the spiritual power and the temporal power, of the Church and the State, of Christianity and nationality. Now this union and solidarity no longer exist. They have been destroyed by the revolt of the Son against the Father, by the false absolutism of the national State which has wanted to be all things while yet remaining alone, in absorbing the authority of the Church, and in suffocating social liberty. This false royalty has engendered false prophets, and the anti-social absolutism of the State has produced, necessarily, the anti-social individualism

---

44 A remarkably concise, accurate statement of the meaning of the *Filioque*.

of progressive civilization. The great social unity, broken by nations and States, cannot be maintained very long by individuals. Human society no longer existing for every man as an integrated totality of which one feels himself a coherent part, social bonds become for the individual only certain exterior and arbitrary limits against which he revolts, and which he ends up suppressing. Then he has liberty, the liberty that death gives to constitutive elements of a body in decomposition. This lamentable image, which the Slavophiles have so much abused against the West, and which has nourished their national pride, should inspire us with quite the opposite sentiments. It is not in the West, it is in Byzantium that the original sin of nationalist particularism and cesaro-papist absolutism have, for the first time, introduced death to the social body of Christ. And the successor of Byzantium now with responsibility is the Russian Empire. And today, Russia is the only country in Christendom where the national State affirms without reserve its exclusive absolutism in making of the Church an attribute of nationality and a passive instrument of the secular government, and where this suppression of divine authority is not even compensated (to the extent it could be) by the freedom of the human spirit.

The second term of the social Trinity – the State or the secular power – due to its intermediate position between the two others, is the principal means either for sustaining or for destroying the integrity of the whole body. In recognizing the principle of unity and of solidarity represented by the Church, and in reducing, in the name of this solidarity, in just measure, all the inequalities produced by the free action of particular forces, the State is a powerful instrument of true social organization. In closing in upon itself, on the contrary, in an absolutism that is isolated and egoist, the State loses its true immutable base and its infallible sanction for social action, and leaves the entire society without defense against "the mystery of iniquity."[45]

Thanks to her historical conditions, Russia presents to us the most complete development, the most pure and most powerful expression of the absolute national State rejecting the unity of the Church and suppressing religious liberty. If we were a pagan people, it would be quite possible for us to fossilize [*cristalliser*] definitively in such a state. But, in the depth of its soul, the Russian people is Christian, and the excessive development which has taken place in it of the anti-Christian principle of the absolute State is the opposite of a true principle: the true principle of a Christian State is that of the Kingship of Christ.[46] That is the *second* principle of the social Trinity, and to manifest it with truth and justice, Russia should, before all, put it in the place where it belongs, recognize it, and affirm it; not as the only and unique principle of our national, *isolated* existence, but as the second of three principal agents of all-embracing social life with which we should be in union. Christian

45   Cf. II Thess. 2:7.
46   Cf. Pius XI, *Quas Primas.*

Russia, in imitating Christ Himself, should submit the power of the State (the Kingship of the Son) to the authority of the Universal Church (the priesthood of the Father), and give a place to societal liberty (action of the Spirit). The Russian empire, isolated in its absolutism, is nothing but a menace to Christianity, a threat of struggles and wars without end. The Russian empire that wishes to serve and protect the universal Church and social organization, will bring to the family of nations peace and blessing.

"It is not good for man to be alone."[47] Nor is it otherwise for a nation. Nine centuries ago were were baptized by St. Vladimir in the name of the fecund Trinity and not in the name of sterile unity. The Russian idea cannot consist in denying our baptism. The Russian idea, the proper role and duty for Russia in history demands of us that we recognize ourselves to be in solidarity with the universal family of Christ and to employ all our national capabilities, all the power of our empire, to the complete realization of the social Trinity, where *every one* of the three principal, co-integrated unities, the Church, the State, and Society, is absolutely free and sovereign, not in separating themselves from one another, in absorbing them or destroying them, but in affirming the absolute solidarity among them. To restore upon the Earth this faithful image of the divine Trinity, this is the Russian idea. And if this idea has no trace of the exclusive and particularist, if it is only a new aspect of the Christian idea itself, if, to

---

47 Gen. 2:18.

accomplish this national mission it is necessary for us to act not *against* the other nations, but *with* them, and *for* them – that is the great proof that this idea is true. For Truth is nothing other than the form of the Good, and the Good knows nothing of envy.

Paris, May 23, 1888

FURTHER READING

SOLOVYOV'S OTHER WRITINGS may be of interest. *La Russie et L'Église Universelle* (1889), and translations of it into English, *Russia and the Universal Church*, are readily available. Certainly worth reading is his intriguing, futuristic story called "A Short History of the Antichrist," also readily available.

For essays on Solovyov and his thought, see, for example:

Frank, S.L., ed., *A Solovyov Anthology*. (London: Saint Austin Press), 2001.

Munzer, Egbert, *Solovyev: Prophet of Russian-Western Unity*. (London: Hollis & Carter), 1956.

Made in the USA
Columbia, SC
03 November 2023